SEAFARER'S JOURNEY

PART 1- THE HELM OF FAITH AND COURAGE

MR. ASHISH RAJENDRA UNAVANE

Contents

Contents

Author's Note

When water flows, like waves in the ocean or the sun sets to the horizon, when the wind on your face from the blue sea and the sky make you breath the freshness of the air and a pen touching the paper to write all the thoughts running in your head with help of words you try to make it known to the world that's pleasure for the writer, expressing his feelings for the reader to go into the wild imagination of the book. The man standing on a beach or in the desert can have a smile on his face or sadness in his eyes regardless of the ocean, sand, wind or sun rays, they are all in the head what you think and what you lead your thoughts to live a life. Choose a better one regardless of past make a better life.

CHOICE IS ALWAYS YOURS

HAVE YOU EVER WONDERED THE LIFE OF A SEAFARER? WHAT HE THINK AND DOES? IS IT ONLY ABOUT GOING NEW PLACES AND HAVING MANY GIRLS AND LUXURIOUS LIFE? LET'S FIND OUT. THE BOOK IS ABOUT THE LIFE OF A SEAFARER AND WRITER HAS MADE IT POETICALLY INTERESTING.

About The Author

Mr. Ashish Rajendra Unavane

I am a 31-year-old Able Seaman working in the merchant navy, I have published before in small competitions in church gatherings but this would be the first on a universal level.

Hope the book is interesting and shares a healthy relation with the readers. It's a memorable and treasured faith written with love for my wife Mrs. Shirly Ashish Unavane, my father Mr. Rajendra Dadoo Unavane, my dearest daughter Miss Erica Ashish Unavane and my mother late. Mrs. Luizamaria Rajendra Unavane.

1. BODY OF CHRIST

Pierced with nails on the cross
My sins are the reason for that loss
You came in flesh to kill it dry
My sins are the reason for that cry

You took away the sins of the world
Only flesh resurrected with time
Everlasting is the word to define
None other than the body of Christ

Predicted way before you took that form
You were always there to inform
Always been in the purest form
When it's Jesus nothing is wrong

You choose not the albatross
Not the raven, the dove was cast
The body indeed died on the cross
But your soul and spirit were never lost

Teaching me what is life
Telling me how to survive
Nothing but give and sacrifice
You proved it and implied

Holy is the word to define
Your body died for soul of mine
Yes indeed resurrected with time
You are my God nothing to hide

Only for gifting me everlasting life
You gave yourself on the cross
My sins are the reason for that cry
I am the reason for that loss

Your flesh and bones your body and soul
Took it all with a cost
Gave me love every drop
I am ready to carry your cross

My resting place all at ones
Giving me hand asking to turn
Away from my sins to you I run
I will be the reason for your fun.

Can't forget your words on cross
Forgiveness for me you only ask
I am the reason for that pain
I will be the reason for your laugh

2. I AM A SAILOR

I am a sailor, yes I am at sea
I was a lover I was a kid,
I wanted all that human need
Yes the rest, yes the peace
I am a sailor, yes am at sea...

Walking the road I had seen
The trees the bird the walking queen,
Friends were few but treasured within,
Now left with a hushing sea and roaring wind
Yes, I am a sailor, and am at sea...

Watching the clock, the date walking,
For the home, I think within,
I think I think I think nothing.
Only the home and queen-sitting
Yes. I am a sailor and am at sea...

Waiting for port for talking
Days are gone without chatting
Technology should improve a little
Letters and posts are not helping
I am a sailor, yes am at sea

With money the pleasure I have with me,
Do not keep me happy within,
Working the months with lonely dreams
I need the love the eyes watching,
Yes, I am a sailor and am at sea...

Holy holy holy the prayers I need,
The water the bread I truly seek,
Faith in you would not go weak
God's BLESSINGS ALWAYS WITH ME,
I am a sailor and am at sea.

3. THE FIRST KISS

If you ask me for a wish
I would go back to the first kiss
My dreams are small with you in it
My treasured ones are few in it

With thoughts and dreams I live
With love and care I sleep
Time is precious with you in it
My smile and my tears are few in it

Little hard work, little pain
That's what it takes, happiness to gain
With grace and hope I look at it
With faith and trust I walk in it

That's what you teach me
With care and love you raised me
I was wrong you made me know
I made you proud, with the kiss you showed

It's time for me to earn now
There is no room for heartburn now
When I failed in love you didn't know
But you were my inspiration to let it go

When I was cheered you were there
When I feared you were there
When you weren't, you were there
You were, you are, you will always be there

Thank you for my first kiss
Must be on my forehead or my cheeks
No I don't remember anything of it
But I am sure you were in it

4. SEAMAN'S LIFE

Seaman needs love, seaman needs wine,
Not working on deck is the only crime,
Seaman is heartless, the seaman is wild,
This is his lust, this is his pride.

Seaman is cold, seaman is salty,
Everything he does is never faulty,
Seaman can swim, seaman can hide,
This is his nature, this is his site.

Alone he lives, alone he cries,
Nine-month at sea changes his mind,
Changes the past, changes the tide,
Everything he saw, may never survive.

His child's cry and his child's laughter,
Awaiting no more for him ever after,
This is the problem, that's the pain,
That's the thing he always gains.

His wife is a sufferer, awaiting no more supper,
Thinking of his safety she always mummer,
That man is her love that man is her life,
Let him come home; let me see into his eyes.

He misses the care, he misses the warmth,
That is the thing he always wants,
The touch the kiss, his only wish,
Everything he gets cannot give him this.

He wants no sea, he wants no ship,
He wants his wife and kid on his side,
To laugh, to cry, to see him die,
That's the seaman, yet he survives.

5. SHE IS MY LOVE SHE IS MY SEA

I love the sea

For I love her as the sea;

She loves me she hates me;

She even cries on me;

She breaks me she hurts me;

She teaches me she treats me;

She gets sad she gets mad;

She even persuades me;

When am at shore she awaits me;

She keeps watch on me she controls me;

When am with someone she is jealous of me

She even warns me

She shows me where I truly belong;

She makes me tough;

She makes me strong;

She doesn't keep me away very long;

I am crowned with her I am bound with her;

Even if I drown I go down with her;

I have no fear;

She'll take me deep in heart of her;

She is my soul she is my guide;

She is my gorgeous she is my pride;

There is nothing that can divide;

She is the only one I call mine;
I love her as she is
She is my precious
She is what she is
She is my love she is mine

6. DARKNESS

Sea has a tendency to be polite
At times the sea can be as cruel as a fight
Can't be sure what's in her mind
No men can ever understand that kind

The darkest nights are peaceful ones
Thoughts and dreams come at ones
It's your plans, life or your loved ones
Sea has a tendency to be a polite one

Flowing waves travel along
The birds the fishes don't take long
To join the journey all night long
Time has the zeal to keep you strong

Sometimes creepy sometimes peace
Depends on mind what it thinks
Steady the course, hold the wheel
Concentration is all it needs

All of sudden it seems harshness
It's like a virus which has no dryness
Darkness is good darkness is healthy
It gives you courage to grow wealthy

Sometimes defined as sadness
Also gives meaning to brightness
It can define thorns and horns
Life has zeal to keep you strong

Being at sea or at shore
Darkness makes you learn more
May be to port or starboard
Staying the course will teach you more

Correct the course colour the canvas
Choose the path with your kindness
Darkness is good indeed healthy
It has zeal to keep you wealthy.

7. IT'S JUST YOU

You are special you are precious
You are only one that matters
You respect me you guide me
You argue me you fight me

You are my friend you are my love
All I give is less you deserve
Still you are here protecting me
Still you are here comforting me

Sometimes I feel this is all enough
I don't want to go I don't want to give up
The time we spend is never enough
But here we are splitting up

Here's the place you truly belong
And here you are to be gone
There's nothing left to be shown
Here are my prayers you live long

Here's the time to let you go
Here's the pain feeding me more
It is you it is just you
All I wanted was to love you

Here I am on the edge you know
Ready to fly ready to blow
It is your wish it's your choice
Want to hold or let it go

No matter what is to come
No matter what is gone
You were,
You are
You will always be the only one...

8. SEAMAN'S STRONG WIFE

Please don't say you love me
It makes us cry
It's my job, it's my life
Today or tomorrow am going to say goodbye

I am a seaman, love!
I belong to the sea
Working for nine months is my duty
I can't wait too long
Baby, you need to be strong

You are my love you are my crush
It might hurt you so much
If this feeling goes too high
I am sure I might die
Staying away, leaving you to survive
It's the only other name for suicide

I will sleep alone
I will eat alone
I will cry alone
I will live alone

You are away or home
It's just you and me
I will be here I guarantee
My every problem is your responsibility

If you mean so
God is our witness
If we keep our vow
God is there to guide us

It takes a strong woman
To be my side
And if it is you
You'll be called a seaman's wife

9. FRIENDS

When I was happy you were there
When I was sad you were there
When I needed you were there
When I didn't you were there

You are my trust you are my guide
There is nothing we can hide
You know me you show me
Even if you try you can't bore me

You are my brother you are my friend
It is only care we can lend
You are my power you are my courage
You are my wisdom you are my strength

We are blessed we have met
Strangest time of despair
Delight and warmth only shared
Rock the ship anyone dare

We are together we will be
When we need here we'll be
We will laugh we will cry
We won't give up we will try

One of us left the course
Finding and chasing lustful whores
Saddle him good with word of prayer
Always ready to boost and cheer

Here's our chance in this life
Meeting you is a delight
Thanks to God for this price
Friends we are on a ride

10. DROWSY BIRD

Drowsy bird flying with us
Dropped on deck with no water
Thirsty and dizzy walking on deck
Leaving few crisscross footsteps

One of us, working guy
Saw this creature couldn't fly
Caught it showed it to us
It was watching with dizziness

We took it to telly room
And surely it wasn't broomed
Gave water some food
That's what we really should

This drowsy little fellow was conscious
Using its wings when someone enters
It's good time when it's around
Sharing sea time roaming around

We named it, we claimed it
It was in our heart and mind
Always peeping at it when passing by
Days and weeks were satisfied

With no sight of land nearby
If we lose, it might die
We were too selfish
Didn't want it to fly

But it is his life, we have to let go
One of us got it out, kissed it goodbye
Wings were flapping as it wanted to run
Away from ship to meet its children

Waited that evening for its return
Cleaning the telly room kept it open
It never returned, it never came back
We are all same working on deck

Hope we were that drowsy bird
We could fly home with conscious
Suddenly the days were hours and hours were minutes
It made us know counting days are only our limits

God as our witness
Loved this creature with guidance
Was it not a drowsy bird?
Reflecting our hearts of innocence

11. CHANGE IN MY SHADOW

There is a change in my shadow
What was yesterday isn't tomorrow
Running on track was fantabulary
Walking on track is mandatory
How life changed is mystery
Sports for me is history

Sportsmanship is seamanship now
It was all green it is all blue now
It happened; I really have no clue how
But there is a change in my shadow
What was yesterday is not tomorrow

Sleeveless, shorts were all I need
Boiler suit, helmet covers me indeed
Spray on deck is from the bow
Spraying water was to cool the ground
Salt was from the sweat of pain
Sea is reason for salty drain

Medals trophies were my treasure indeed
Money is the reason now it seems
Clearing stones to run on track
It's all rust for the deck
How life changed is mystery
Sports for me is history

Sleeping was must before the big game
Sleeping on deck is now a shame
Speed was only mean of vocabulary
Speaking much isn't my category

Hope life gives me chance again
To walk on grass and run again
Only fear is one for me
I should cope up with myself again

There is a change in my shadow
In me it's a wondering sorrow
How life changed is still a mystery
Sports indeed is my history

12. HELPLESS MERCHANTS

Lives were floating with birds around
Paid with pennies worth at all?
Waves were friends just along
Talking to us all night long

There was a boat following us
Hearts were raised high at first
We might see some action around
That was the sound on piracy ground

We started scanning all around
Eyes were sharp right round
Guns were ready hands were strong
We were in mist with pirates around

Engines high fingers crossed
Speeding ourselves fourteen knots
We might see some action around
That was the sound on piracy ground

Helpless merchants with guns three or two
Strength of our ship was twenty-one crew
Hoses were rigged razors too
Sandbags placed covering through

Time was slow ready to shoot
Did we see a warship too?
Waves were noisy splashing through
Helpless merchants with guns three or two

There was a time
Both were aligned
With our speed we went through
Sailing boat and warship crew

There might be a fight
There might be a war
9 months at sea
Let us stay strong

We passed miles from there too
Just to live a day or two
Strength of our ship remained twenty-one crew
Helpless merchants with guns three or two

13. THEY ARE SEAMEN ATLAST

Splash of sea hush of wind,
Awake at last awake at last
Making the crew awake at last,
Rocking ship hiding moon
Watching the sea awake at last,

All you see is black sea
All you see is black sky
Boosting all lads
Keep the powder dry
Here are all awake at last,

Dreams of home wants of life
Making all do an unwanted try
Keeping the crew awake at last

This is your home; this is your choice,
Don't give up lads money is price,
Heaving hard heaving strong
Keeping the crew awake at last

Sweat of pain blood of sorrow
Will bare your fruit some day tomorrow
Awake at last awake at last
Keep yourself awake at last,

Safety of ship safety of crew
Is upon what you have to do,
Don't be weak don't be slack
These words keep the crew
Awake at last awake at last,

End is near don't you fear,
Storm won't last against your gear,
The birds are here the rays are here,
The time to sleep is very near,
This is the hope keeping all crew
Awake at last

At last the end of storm
Just then it was very wrong,
The hull was crack and ship going down,
Here's the crew again,
Keeping themselves awake at last

Not losing hope not giving up,
It's seaman's nature it's seaman's chance
Given up hope until end
Trying to live their exhausted breath
All of them were saved at last.

14. YOU ARE UNIQUE

Light do not have shadow
But is the only reason to create one,
Time does not have life
But shadows to make yours a better one
Emotions do not drain
But are always to shed upon,
You are unique trust me on that one

Life can be painful,
Have a purpose to live on
Be a better man be a better person
Not compared to anyone,
But to yourself past one
Always wash and scrub
All that shit you stepped on

Remembering them won't change it,
Learn from them and move on,
I know saying is easy
But tough to act upon
Only solution to that is
Accept and have a life to move on
You are unique trust me on that one

Keep the light on your front and shadow behind
Take the next step head-on
Perfect life is always a mess
Pursuing it is always a quest
Ask for it and you shall receive
It all depends on how you request
You are unique trust me on that one

Sometimes change is a good one.
From all that you have gone through,
Doesn't has to be the next one,
Growing old is not purpose of life,
Find a new to create one,
Even the most popular is a lonely one,
Right steps he takes make him a better one,

Do things that make you proud
Motivation doesn't need a source
Still a lonely, even in the crowd
Choices you make to hold on or move on
Make you a unique trust me on that one.

15. FACE

A person has many faces,
Depends on what all he faces
Life shows him different phases
Adapts the nature of those phases,

The way he talks
The way he looks
The way he smiles or cries
Are all adapted from those phases,

No am not talking about ugly or beauty
All are made with God's glory
But how we behave and act
Adapted are all from those phases

You like a person or you hate
Attraction towards him makes you amaze,
Yes the looks are in place
But that's not only what you gaze,

Character of the person is what you trace
Judging a person with his face
His trust in you can be replaced
All depends on choices both make

You are either praised or disgraced
The consequences of choices you make
It is visible on your face
Judging others is a disgrace

Memories are all that remains
Cherish them in heart and your brain
Sometimes joy sometimes pain
Adapted the nature of those phase

It is all visible on your face
Makeup can't hide nor remain
Watch yourself closely
Choices you make are on your face

Face changes yes with age
Grows with the choices that you make
Emotions of joy and of that pain
Always raised on your face

16. VOICE OF A SPORTSMAN

Running wasn't just fun for me
It was strength, heartbeat for me
The brown ground, wet grass
Boosting coach, cheering mates
All of these energized me
Winning or losing didn't matter much
Giving everything on the track was the must
Grasping for air the loud shout
That was my strength, heartbeat for me
Running wasn't just fun for me
The ground was my bed
The grass was my pillow
It did say hi when I said hello
It helped me to win

It teaches me to loose
Number four lane
Never give up attitude
Short pants, sleeveless shirts
Unknown wounds, dripping blood
Shaky legs, speeding time
The gun shot, finishing line
Running wasn't just fun for me
It was strength, heartbeat for me
Challenge myself was the game
Sometimes winning made my name
That was left with no pain
Voice of wind cheering the gain
Guilt of losing still hurts me
In my brain it still burns me
Practice gave me purpose
It was all like a circus
It took away all my pain
There was never a lonely rain
Running gave me happiness
A source of taking out all sadness
When everything was set and done
There was only one thing to learn
Those medals trophies were just for show
The real thing was on the ground
When they said on your mark, set and go
Running wasn't just fun for me
It was strength, heartbeat for me.

17. BEING THERE

Nothing is more important than being there
Life gives you chance to love and care
Life even give chance to forgive and forget
But the only key to all is being there

Chances are to be loved
Getting to being someone's special
Influence others to stay and flourish
Sighing like breeze for being there

We fall for people every day
We labour ourselves every day
How far you go to test your strength
There is nothing import then being there

There is no point in that role
Sighing in anger for not being there
Chances are to be alone
Optimism and dreams you pour there

Rocking the ship with zero speed
Sometimes dizzy, making you kneel
Pleasing and peaceful, making you feel
Only the memories of being there

Phase of hopeless and mere oblivion
Straighten your voice and your vision
Steady your course hold on that wheel
For yourself you have to be there

Time is too short time is precious
Courage you want no despair
Life is ones believe you can
There is nothing more important than being there

18. RARE INCIDENT

Archived story for on board few
Digging my past with young three or two
Before the time of ECDIS and Radar
Paper charts stacked weren't new

Drills were tossed off the ground
Ships speed 12 knots over the ground
Reaching port was a dream comes true
Yes we did in months three or two

Technology changed the news wasn't slow
Rare incident that shivered the core
Secrets of industry are on platform few
Controlling the damage of mistakes new

Families unaware for the safety of crew
Network jammed for any false news
Known to the wise and experts few
Loaded vessel grounded with all the crew

Temporary welding by divers under
Lifted the ship at dry dock afloat
After the tugs pulled us with time
After the cargo discharged of course

The cracks were seen under the keel
The bottom tank were ruptured still
At the float the oil was spilled
Shore crew did the repair of course

We worked our time and went ashore
After a long in a bar downtown
Cheers to standing on the unwavering ground
Yes we did waited too long

Served together shared few beers
Don't know if alive all this years
Some experience with on-board crew
Ship mates sail or retired over the years

Going home was a dream comes true
Leaving the ship for joined new crew
Loved and cared by families too
It was a memorable struggle we went through

19. FREEDOM

No right or wrong in navigation
Perspective changes with every situation
Boundaries are set ahead for you
Gives different scenario ahead of you

Name, religion, personality is judged of you
Make sure no borders are made for you
Win the hurdles from heart and brain
Does it not mean freedom for you?

Imaginary lines are guarded from you
Crossing them is real friction for you
Scaling your scull and strength
Sufferance gets the better of you

State of mind that's holding you
Belief and faith of what you do
Challenging them is trembling you
Digging in more is freedom for you

Purpose of life searching you
Alone or along depends on you
Finding and knowing the ultimate truth
Does it not mean freedom for you?

Too much of traffic ahead of you
Change the course wouldn't you?
Path is just guiding you
Time and tide won't be same but new

Discovering new horizon and goal
Making them part of your own
Isn't it really exiting for you?
Is that not freedom for you?

20. TALK

Mamma you need to talk
You need to walk
Mamma don't lose hope
You need to talk

Lifting you like a baby
Climbing on the rock
Time flew too soon
Watching the clock

Tell me what you need
Tell me what you want
Everything I can loose
Time won't stop

Mamma you need to try
You can't give up
Mamma don't say you can't
You are my rock

You made me grow
You made me strong
But for you am weak
I can't see you drawn

Why can't you bite?
Why can't you swallow?
Don't say sorry
Nothing is wrong

Bruises on the tongue
Swelling on the cheeks
Everything is tasteless
Going through your lips

Tell me you want to live
Tell me you won't stop
Hold my hand
Let's pray come-on

Why are you silent mamma?
Is there any pain
Tell me talk to me
You need to talk

21. MINUTES

The moon and the stars were gazing so
Watching the ship rocking its course
Minutes of peace to cherish you know
Few drops of rain maintaining the flow

The shine on deck, not the metal afloat
But the smile and laughter keeping the glow
The bell were rung and a song was played
A voice of an angel heard from the shore

Mothers memories and fathers care
Daughters' love and wife's prayer
Strengthening the tide with no regrets
Keeping me boosted with no despair

Through the valleys and the cities
Through the labour and the pities
Pause of a time to think
Clearing the fog and the white snow

Getting the chill freezing the toe
Keeping the faith as the wind blow
Within the heart waiting with hope
Waiting to pour out and disclose

Losing the fear courageous throw
Grasping for air story untold
Like a chapter to be unfold
There goes the minutes splashing the core.

22. CHANGE OF TIDE

All dreams are getting its shape
With some cracks in its place
Going home to see some change
Feels complete to have all it takes

Sons' marriage in time left few
House was breathless shifted to new
Fulfilling her dreams come true
For her they were not all but very few

Mom's funeral was unexpected
Last I met was unpredicted
Struggle in bed wasn't enough
The machine the air couldn't keep up

Silence of the sea change to roar
Incomplete without her is the shore
Having someone in life is much more
Trusting someone other than your own

Woman of the house is changed now
Expected with my child she is now
Filling all things making new now
Moving ahead is all I can do now

Taking moms place isn't expected
Keep the spirit make it grow now
The house has been sad for too long
Fill it with joy only you can do now

I know its hard am at sea
Have my child take care of thee
Few more years let us grow
Happiness for you I want to see

I know for you it's only me
I can't give up on my responsibility
This tide is a different reality
Only thing I ask is patience with me.

Past is not going to change
It will be in memory lane
Smile and pray for the upcoming gift
Trying best to accept the change

23. OCEAN

I crave nothing but only peace
Lust and love a thin line between
At the heat of equator crossing
Oceans belly I want dive and swim

Saving lives when sirens ring
You are the only oceans queen
No flesh on earth could possibly give
A pleasure to serve the floating queen

Family and friends make heart rising
Echoes from them are miles to reach
Part of the ship part of the crew
Dwelling the ocean with only peace

Only desire I have is for this hush
Work on deck had no end or rush
On which even the moon had a crush
All the water around was so shush

The song of death turned to musical beat
With those creatures who dwell within
Music to ears your vocal beats
Even the shadows of death are so pleased

The clouds of rain are to follow
The sweat of pain is to narrow
Peaceful smile gives this cold breeze
Vapour of sweat is nowhere to be seen

End of the voyage is near it seems
Golden shore is visibly reach
Ready to berth flake all moorings
This smile on face is hard to squeeze

24. PRINCESS AND THE SERVANT

Daughter of the king and queen
Princess of the most adventurous thing
Filled with love and lots of thrill
Kept in the heart for singing

Crushed under a giant I shall go
Might hurt the princess holding on though
Two choices, how should I know?
Hurting my princess wasn't my goal

Scattered indeed my choice was so
Under the giant-like sand you know,
Crying was the princess watching the show
Why did the servant have to go?

Blessed the princess shattering though
The servant used magic before he goes
She couldn't fly the highest sky
Or swim the deep as all know

Her every smile was a gift
Fulfilled her only wish
Picked the sand yes she did
Kissed the jar filled with it

Tears of her frost the jar
Wanted a cure for healing the scar
Until then need to secure
Why did the servant have to go?

Came a man with crippled toe
Long bearded, white as snow
Shinning head with two sprouts though
Fighting each other when the wind blow

Blood most pure will lift him sure
On his feet and his toes,
Gave the princess some cure
None but the humble, he said so

More then a friend can't let go
Asked the man did you know
What was he, wondering so?
Not just a servant, he said so

The sea was his blood,
The crew was his soul
The ship was his body
Steady on a course

She was far from the shore
Picked the jar and let's go
Collected wood on the way
As the old man said so

On a horse tic tact toe
Smiled on the way there's hope
With a man guiding so
Magic made the whole land glow

Sailing some ship she had thought
It was her command until she wants
Finished was the story was it not
Depends on princess smiled she on

Jar was frost with her tears
Watched it daily didn't cheer
Finding the cure picking things told
On the way to the shores

Later she got what's the trick
Choice was hers always has been
Like a ship that need repair
Keeping the servants well being

Hurting herself wasn't the choice
If she did magic was lost
Poor little princess was the crew
Wanted the sea and some wood

Collect she did all of it
Old man also showed some tricks
On the way, yes he did
Shore was near could feel it

Broke the jar dropped with things
Didn't notice it but smiling
The breeze and river was flowing
Turned the servant into a prince

Strong like a ship
Gentle as the sea
Courageous was his spirit
Caring was his soul

Married she did lived with him
Prince he became she turned him
She has all the wanted means
To turn a man as slave or as prince

Heart of her was filled with thrill
Choice is hers always it is
She was daughter of the king and queen
Princess of the most adventurous thing

25. IT'S TIME TO GO NOW

It's time to go now it's time to leave
One day ashore 100 years at sea
With memories love and care with me
It's time to go now it's time to leave

Your smile your eyes watching me
Your love your care protecting me
Staying is the heart really needs
But it's time to go now it's time to leave

I never met you before I never saw you before
And here I am nothing left as before
You are in my heart you are in my mind
There is nothing from you I want to hide

I want to know you I want to hear you
I want time only to love you
And hear I am with left nothing
Only time to go the time to leave

SEAFARER'S JOURNEY

It's time to go now it's time to leave
I want you in real not in my dreams
This is the song I only sing
As we heave the anchor and moorings

Back to sea back to ship
And the same working ring
Thinking and dreaming I spend the way
Again the same counting days

Your smile your words are with me
Safe and care be with thee
Only thing remains is memories
It's time to go now it's time to leave

26. MEMORIES

Things change things do change
People die people go away
Ground, trees, building all change
Only thing remains is memories

The stick the cycle the road
The classroom alleyway the corridor
Her eyes her smile her voice
All are just memories
All that remains is memories

Only thing that matters were you
My wants my likes were very few
Why me, was your first question
Answering that call was only imagination

No I am not missing
I am not crying
Just thinking of what we were
Great was the time together

This is what I am when I think of you
Words for love are very few
Thoughts and dreams are as morning dew
With silence and peace it comes and shows

With love there are no boundaries
Care and love are just responsibilities
All that remains is memories
All that matters is memories

She is in care of God
She at peace
Her lucky lips her caring voice
They all are just memories

Building me up from innocence
Towards the life of foolishness
All that remain is memories.
All that matters is memories.

27. NAME

Every face has a name
Every phase has its frame
Your is the most precious one
Haven't seen yet
You are yet to be born

Future of my house
Next generation of my race
Nothing else I want to gaze
You are one of many God's grace

Couldn't be there when you are born
My life is such there's nothing wrong
I am going to be your father
Yet haven't thought of a perfect name

World is beautiful God has made
Some bad too don't be afraid
Mom is there to protect
Dad is there to guide
Just make sure to be brave

Your future is in good hands
You have a shelter and family that rise
Many are not lucky to have what it takes
Be strong be humble don't be a disgrace

Strongest of wind we will face
Together as my parents kept until date
Love you my child keep smile on your face
Will do everything I can to keep you safe

Always correct yourself make mistakes
Sailors' strength runs through your veins
Nothing is easy without pain
Cast off the ropes and set you course
The ocean is big enough let us sail.

28. WHITE OWL

Sign of prosperity and messenger of peace
Happiness on the way all started to speak
A white owl height not more than feet
Resting his wings and taking a sit

Is it my God speaking with me?
He has a unique way you see
Why? From where is this delivery?
Is it some news from family?

Gave some food when the bell ring
Thought he had plans to stay the din
It did fly over the ship and sheen
The birth of my child was next seen

Afraid and praying were all that evening
Only I was the one to talk and sing
I wonder if he ate before leaving
Few days the owl was wondering

All of this was supernatural thing
My daughter is my mother all wondering
No that's not what my bible teach
But for sure my daughter is unique

Get together time for party
All did sing for my baby to wish
Life has its way to open its chits
Another turn of direction and twist

Long way to sail waiting to kiss
Will you have some chubby cheeks?
Lifting you up can be a trick
Dreaming to hold your tiny feet's

Time for me is slow and stiff
Patience is all I have to keep
Work on deck is little weak
All are the memories to store and click

29. DAUGHTER

Focus of my heart was on your mother
Her pain her strength and time was a fear for me
To know that you are a girl is a price for me
Now that you are born it's a surprise for me

Greatest fear isn't that you are a girl child
But can I be a father to you my beautiful child
Every girl I met were in my brain that moment
Can I give you my time was a fear for me?

You have a nose of your mother
Her struggle her love is everything for me
To know that you look like her is a price for me
Now that you are born it's a surprise for me

Future is running in my head now
Your school, your friends and marriage is all there now
I will be your strength on the way
Nothing else on earth is important for me

Being far at sea is tough for me
Being a father is a great responsibility
Now that you are born it's a challenge for me
Your mother and you are gift for me

You are a sailor's child
Strength and patience in you is from me
To give you time is a prayer for me
Hope we make some good memories

Hard work and labour is chosen for me
With God I walk, he has been there for me
Forgiveness is all I ask from him for me
Now that you are born it's a new turn of life for me

30. SILENCE

It's been years unwritten,
There are words unveiled and hidden,
Just when everything felt forgotten,
There is this age of foolishness.

For now the voice is a captive bird
The energy the power is getting some rust
Silence of maturity covered with dust
Unveiled itself from dawn to dusk

Miles away from the shore
Strength by the age of technology
Middle of innocence and maturity
There was this age of foolishness.

Darkest clouds filled with tears
Trumpet of patience within me
Innocence fighting the maturity
It's not about my time and me

Focus on the beginner is must
Everything is new in your crust
Learning to crawl feeding on breast
Teaching me to take my first step

In my head there is a storm
Shaving and trimming all negativity
Silence is key for some clarity
Here is the age of maturity

Yes you are the one teaching me
The age of innocence reminding me
Empowered by the strength of pen
The age of foolishness covered by maturity

31. SEARCH

Moon is crawling in the clouds you see
While this silent sea is watching me
Gift from God blessing thee
Just love for your mother and me

Mammas hand holding thee
Little other hand is searching me
Hearing my voice she looks for me
Does she even remember me?

Looking at mamma kissing thee
Smiling at her when she talks of me
Strangest way of loving me
Do you even remember me?

All about you is stored in me
Trusted your mamma only me
Strange connection this technology
Hearing and watching only thee

Gibberish you speak when spoken of me
Babbling with mamma she keeps telling me
She is a strong mother gave birth to you
Holding together our house and you

Grandma from heaven blessing you
Grandpa is there to entertain you
He is the one who raise you and me
Smart man in house little old you see

Searching for strength holding me
Asking the question within me
Does she even know me?
Does she even remember me?

32. TREASURE

What is a treasure if not the time?
The precious slipping is one of a kind
Glittering gold that loose not its pride
Every craving and lust is no match behind

Handing over the watch to generation in line
Apart from each other, the family line
Faith and love is all that survives
Passed on to the next with all the time

Growing with hate won't be delight
Shortens the clan with none behind
No tales to create or to share
Rage and war leaves no one to shine

Falling and choosing can't be avoided
Learn to grow with some darkness and void
Losing the essence for your own
Teach the next to be strong with time

Treasure which even the pirates can't find
Can't have more nor theft or bribe
It's not less but perfect kind
Some have plenty but do not mind

Can't take with you after the life
The wealth and fame all left behind
The treasure takes all everything
Whatever I have is never mine

It's like the sand slipping from the hands
Catching up is something none can survive
Degrees and safety is one way to climb
Unique treasure indeed is called the time

33. GLORY TO THE LORD

From the psalms of David from the songs of praise
From the book of life from the sound of grace
A beautiful hymn a melody peacefully rose
Giving glory to the Lord the dance in pace

The birds aligned to the sunset shine
The song was sung for the humble and kind
The servants were jolly in the peaceful church
The Lord was pleased by the worshipers

Every creature with cords or without
Praised the Lord all that sprouts
Isn't it what the bible teaches?
With the words of praise no doubt

Every journey set sail the course
Wonderful writings for the ears of course
My God is praised in the oceans deep
From the dreadful sorrow to the joyful thrill

Follow the path promises to keep
We all have his arms in paradise to sleep
Follow his lead to the pastures green
He leads the path for all the sheep

Every unsung has his deeds
In the blood of Christ it was cleansed
In the shadow of death or the brightness of light
Protected, comforted and covered indeed

34. UNIQUE RELATION

Can I write what a brother does?
Do I know how a sister cares?
Sharing and growing in one shelter
Protecting and nourishing each other

Born from a different relationship
First guard to a scared sister
Second mother to a baby brother
This is one of the relations to treasure

No the words are too weak
This connection is prestige
Regardless of the physic
Two souls cherished together

No no the toys are way apart
Cloths to wear and some bruise to bear
I guess its human nature
Partner in crimes blaming each other

Do I know of this bonding?
Core reason of this grounding
I think I could only guess
Uniqueness between the opposite sexes

Teaching them honour and respect
To keep the sacredness of each other
Parents have the responsibility to care
To keep the innocence of the gender

Wickedness and sickness sometime to share
Few years apart crying with despair
Children are the treasure of wonderland
Creators' blessings to the parents who have

35. SHOOTING STAR

A meteoroid that lost its track
Speeded far to its dreadful death
On a peaceful night of an open sky
Came broken detached from an asteroid

One closed eyes the other gave a sigh
Stared the ship that went by
Keeping lookout not standby
Altering the course as required

One had faith and one enjoyed the view
Amazing sight for the watch keepers two
On the ship safely navigating through
Both gave a smile in that dark looking a minute or two

Sporadic meteor or the shooting star
One scratched his beard and other his scar
Prayer for the loved with hopes a few
Other looked and said nature is so beautiful

Was it the Zeus throwing stones?
Pointing it gave bad luck on those
Two unique points had distinct view
Spark comes from faith and knowledge too

The smile of one had its clue
The other focused on the passing Cruz
Navigating safely with caution
The nigh of watch keepers just went shush

36. RUSTED MEDALS

Those are the metal plates kept stacked in dust
Boosting the spirit from my memory lane
Scraping and screaming under the rust
My name written in bold under its crust

Those were shiny someday, wrapped, sometimes gazed
Smiling, sometimes cry upon the events and days
Like a ship which did its dedicated purpose
With its glory hypnotised and amazed

Words of the nursing mother to the infant
Your father's passion is not waste
It made a new horizon on the lane
Cannot be forgotten in this fast lane

But those rusted medals are rotten and stained
Ribbon that hung is shredded the link that joint is corroded
Juggling the box makes them awake
Breaks the rust which accumulate

Should it be hidden in a dark place?
Or on the shelf shined to gaze
Like in a museum, polished and cased
Does it matter, why to chase?

Looks like the sweat is drained
Tears and blood washed in the rain
Borders are broken like useless fishplate
It may spoil the entire place

It's ok for the oil spill on the ship need to contain
Sometime takes days to regain
There are young do not demotivate
It's like catching the running train

Some unfocused events from past memory lane
Get up, never give up, those might be rusted
But achieved in your game
And still on it there is your name

Those rusted medals do not decide your fate
Rebuilt with love and care that is our faith
You will be bullied you will be played
Time and God is your witness
Those might be rusted
But are achieved by your hard work and pain

37. DECISIONS

Joining the sea was a bold decision
Was not at all easy for the only son
More than a decade sailing the ocean
Where time flied is the question?

Signing the contract a shaky decision
Catching a flight had its turbulence
Responsibility on the teenage shoulders
Choices I made had its conclusions

So much went by over the years
There were smiles and some tears
Oceans breeze holds my fear
Splashing seas as the companions

Defining home is confusion
Spent most of life at the ocean
So many colours caught the eyes
Floating jail as time went by

Each sign-off had a relief
Made me wonder what to believe
More than a decade sailing the ocean
Are there any friends is the question?

As the compass points direction
Life leaded its own correction
Sometime magnet caught the attraction
Goals of life had its distractions

All the journey achieved and lost
Throughout the way time was cost
Loosing and finding the loved ones
Breaking and moulding self-conscious

Choice to stay or make decision
Beginning a new journey is an option
Following the way with all confession
Staying the course or changing direction

Husband and father are tags on me
Responsibilities with sailing the sea
God must have plans for this servant
Leading my way to a new direction

38. TRUST

Steps to trust are always cautious
They can lead to glory or pain
Trusting blind isn't an option
Choices are always there before us
Element of surprise is unique
Sold your soul isn't it Faustus?

Steps to trust are gambling and losses
They can endure the entire corpus
Works like the oil and saw-dust
Spillage only incinerate the existence
Element of love is unique
Wasn't the death of Romeo and Juliet?

Trusting blind is never an option
Even the family can be caucus
Centuries have passed teaching us
Politics is out of my jurisdictions
There must be some maquiladoras
Shut by the lack of faith and trust

Both of them go hand in hand
Lacking them is pain and death
Can't sail the blue without trust
Isn't it Captain and Mr Steward?
Ships metal only grew layers of rust
There are sunken ships throughout ocean

We make mistakes that we learn
Holding on them is not so fun
Living a healthy life is so simple
Make more mistakes on the run
Repeating them aren't an option
Challenging self and learn from them

This book is just a step ahead
Walk with a seafarer did we not?
Hope you all enjoyed till now
Making it fun, am I not?
Drinks and cheers way along
Faith and love come beyond

I am just a common seaman
It's only a job that cometh
Chipping the metal
Cleaning the stores
Heaving up the anchor
Casting off the ropes

SEAFARER'S JOURNEY

Sailing for a new journey
Sailing beyond new horizon
Sea is too vast to end
Seafarer's journey has just begun
Let's search for more buoyage
Bon appetite and bon voyage

39. LESSONS TO GAIN

Farsight star has its own glory
Marks you gave didn't define my story
Made me stronger with each tide
The life I chose has redefined

I lost your care I didn't mind
Moulding and forcing me taking its own time
Chemistry and trigonometry has its own flow
Yes it's used somewhere but I don't know

People who used it are well mannered and kind
That doesn't mean I am a different kind
All that teaching is only to make you smarter and wise
Learning is a process not a stamp on our kind

Gender is limited to sexual desire
That shouldn't stop you for thinking higher
Save yourself for the spouse
That is the teaching every religion shouts

Focus on your faith God will guide
All earthly pleasure is limited to time
Everything you know even the religion and faith
Too much of anything is either blind or pressure to brain

All the memories slowly lost at sea
Blurriness of eyes made the world hazy
Those path lead to glory or pain
Wrong or right are the choices to gain

Limit your pressure or go insane
Courage you get stronger the faith
Not in witchcraft or any such games
Destiny needs patience and faith

Every poem in this book is teaching the same
Hold on to the helm of faith
Strengthen you courage
Focus only on the choices that you make

With its own boredom has a lesson too
Hope for the journey to continue
Written about it by a common sailor
With hope and love to continue